THE ABSOLUTELY ESSENTIAL GUIDE TO MEETING SURVIVAL

By Vic Parrish

Illustrated by Stephen Jackson

COPYRIGHT ©2018 by Vic Parrish

Printed and bound in the United States of America. All rights reserved. No part of this book may be copied or transmitted in any form or by any means, electronic or mechanical, including photocopying, record, or by any information storage or retrieval system – except by a reviewer who may quote brief passages and in a review to be printed in a magazine, newspaper or by the Web without permission in writing by the copyright holder.

For more information contact:
Vic Parrish

Vic.parrish@yahoo.com

ISBN-13: 978-1985069084
ISBN-10: 1985069083

For additional copies please contact the author as above.

ACKNOWLEDGEMENTS

To those poor souls lost over the years to the black holes known as meetings - VP

To anyone who has ever had to sit in a meeting with S.K. or L.R. for you have truly suffered. - **SJ**

THE ABSOLUTELY ESSENTIAL GUIDE TO MEETING SURVIVAL

This guide is provided in a humanitarian effort to improve the lives of millions around the globe. Utilize the information contained herein judiciously and wisely, for misuse or abuse of these techniques could result in increased vigilance on the part of superiors, thereby complicating any future efforts on your part, as well as making the implementation of these methods difficult for others. Just like the child in grade school whose behavior ruins recess for the entire class, you do not want to be known as a spoiler, possibly subjecting yourself to retribution, both psychological and physical, to say nothing of professional repercussions.

THE PROBLEM

There is an unfortunate occurrence that most adults must face for which childhood has left them completely unprepared. Educational organizations have failed us in this area, and that includes the hallowed institutions of higher learning. With the money and effort expended to ostensibly prepare people for life in the real world, it is an appalling state of affairs that exists. I am speaking, of course, of meeting attendance.

With the frequency of meetings confronting employees in the workplace, it is surprising that this subject is not broached in the course of our education. We learn most of the basics necessary for performing in our chosen professions, but preparation for something that takes up such a large part of our work lives is sadly lacking. Whether you are new to the workforce, or a long-suffering veteran, it is hoped that this modest tutorial will, in its small way, help alleviate this terrible shortcoming.

It is important to note that there are meetings you will be called upon to attend that have value and meaning. HA! Just kidding. Almost every single meeting to which you have been invited (compelled?) to be present will be tedious, useless and a huge waste of everyone's time, especially yours. Unless it's an announcement of ridiculously huge bonuses, long-deserved raises or promotions, extravagant parties catered and completely paid for by the company, or a public shaming of the hated section manager, it's going to be a disaster. Let's look at this more closely:

1) <u>Meetings are called to give you the illusion of input when everything has actually already been decided.</u>
   You read that correctly. Your opinion doesn't matter. The issue was settled some time ago, maybe during a few holes of golf or perhaps while downing a cocktail or two. Imagine your boss with a big Cohiba cigar, lighting it with a $50 bill and chuckling with a gaggle of lickspittles over the new plan to rearrange the office layout in order to help them reach the door a few seconds earlier at quitting time. In the meeting there will be copious talk about efficiency, ergonomics, perhaps even *feng shui*. Your deluded coworkers will earnestly discuss these

matters as though what they are saying will make any difference at all. Watch for the subtle ways that those in charge lead the conversation to the predetermined decisions. Note the naïve excitement in the voices of the people convinced that they are helping to improve the organization. See the practiced way in which the boss concedes value in an opinion expressed, but also raises seemingly valid reasons as to why the offered solution is unworkable. An experienced supervisor will be laughing inside as the group is directed to the preferred suggestion, while the attendees imagine the suggestion to have been arrived at through sincere debate. See the glee in the eyes of the meeting leader as success in deception is achieved. This is almost sport enough to make a meeting worthwhile. Almost.

An experienced supervisor will be laughing inside

2) <u>The meeting you are in will invariably lead to another meeting.</u>
That's right; this very important meeting that has taken such a large chuck of your precious time will in fact *resolve nothing.* After hours of discussion, debate and possibly terroristic threats, it will be decided to table the issue and "approach it again with fresh eyes". You will all leave the room exhausted and seeking solace in various vices. Perhaps thoughts of murder will dance around in the minds of several of you. That future meeting will be a rehash of everything already discussed, and then a decision MAY be made, if you're lucky (please see #1 above).

There will be more meetings.

3) <u>The email announcing the meeting will contain everything necessary for the decision to be made.</u>
All the information relevant for the decision will have been laid out already. A simple vote button at the top of the email would have sufficed. In a sadistic expansion of that, the meeting will include a word-for-word rereading of the email, in as dry and monotone a voice as possible. What's that? You're capable of reading on your own? You obviously aren't a team player. There will be an email later regarding mavericks such as yourself - followed by a meeting to ensure that everyone understands expectations.

The over detailed meeting agenda.

4) <u>Your presence at the meeting is unnecessary.</u>

15 minutes into it you will begin to wonder "why do they need ME?" as the topics wander to every subject under the sun EXCEPT for things that involve you. Not an accountant? The most recent overhead figures will be primary. Perhaps you work in IT? Technology will be conspicuously absent from the agenda. "This is a sales problem!" your mind will scream. "I'm in data entry!" Surely that's not true, you argue. I'm being called upon to give an important report! You must be referring to the one that is scheduled for the fourth hour of the session. In the meantime, please sit still and give your full attention to janitorial services talking about bathroom tissue usage. It's for the good of everyone. And

while you're at it, please help yourself to the dried pastries and browning fruit being thoughtfully provided. But not too much! There's that toilet paper issue…

5) <u>The person most needed for the meeting can't make it.</u>
Well, as long as we're all here anyway, let's discuss the problem with morale.

With the deck stacked so completely against you, it is a matter of self-preservation rather than idleness that requires matters to be taken into your own hands. As you read further, do so with a sense of pride and dignity, firm in the belief that you are engaging in an act of noble defiance. Any suggestion that following these guidelines is passive-aggressive, immature or juvenile may be safely dismissed as the self-delusional defensive hysterics of slaves to a repressive system.

Thoughtfully provided pastries and fruits.

AVOIDANCE

The best way to survive meetings, of course, is to **avoid them entirely**. The rest of this essay is superfluous if this can be achieved. On some rare occasions the right blend of circumstances and forethought may happily result in a plausible reason/justification/excuse that can free you from the soul-crushing misfortune before you. Let's examine a small sampling. Feel free to invent your own, but use your head before using your mouth.

- "I'm expecting a call from (important client/partner)." If you ordinarily have no dealings with people at this level, do not use. It's just ridiculous for a low-ranking worker, for example, to employ such a cover.
- "The Director has asked for these reports by the end of business today." This can easily backfire if the Director is going to be in attendance, or if you are actually responsible for said reports and they do not appear at the appointed time. It also invites further questions regarding the nature of such reports.

- "My dentist appointment is in 20 minutes." If you've got the sick leave to cover it, this is an excellent excuse. You're out for the rest of the day if Dame Fortune has smiled upon you and the meeting is in the afternoon. You can prepare for this by making random comments about your teeth early in the week.
- "The printer is acting up. Give me a few minutes to pull these documents together and I'll be right there." This will only buy you time, not get you out completely. Still, any time away is respite from the torture.
- "I have explosive diarrhea." The dangers of this one don't really need to be remarked upon, do they?

If you find success with these tactics or others, congratulations! Alas, avoidance is difficult for many reasons, so you will more than likely be put into a position to utilize the information that follows.

Dental appointments are a great excuse to get out of a meeting.

SEATING

Nothing is more important in meeting survival than choice of seat. Nothing. Poor choices invite scrutiny of your activities, and scrutiny is your biggest obstacle. No matter your skill and experience in deflecting or avoiding attention, sitting in the wrong place will render this very, very difficult. Proximity to meeting leaders, invasive or inquisitive coworkers, brown-nosing employees or avenues of entrance/egress will severely impact your ability to perform the kinds of tasks necessary for your sanity. Practice and perfect this skill first, before attempting to move on to the more advanced procedures. You have been warned.

Poor seating choices invite scrutiny.

LOCATION

There are two basic locations for meetings: the auditorium-type setting and the meeting room. This guidebook does not discuss the individual meeting, where only two to four people are present. Those circumstances are fraught with peril by their very nature, and the fact that you are in one of them, particularly of the one-to-one sort, may indicate that you are already in over your head, and attention to the proceedings is of utmost importance. This cannot be emphasized enough.

One-on-one meetings are particularly perilous.

AUDITORIUMS

The auditorium provides the best of environments for practicing meeting survival. It is probable that there are large numbers of people involved, and, like any herd animal, your chances for being specifically singled out for attention are correspondingly lower. The knowledge that an auditorium is the chosen site can justifiably be cause for elation; this is a good place for amateurs to practice, but even then overconfidence can be deadly. The nature of the meeting may help to clue you in to your boundaries and limitations. As in church, the best location is in the very back, at the end of the row. This puts you as far as possible from the speaker(s) and from any annoyingly toadying coworkers, most of whom sit near the front to be seen by the upper echelon and given approving nods. Distant placement allows you to convincingly maintain an air of interest while employing the methods we will be discussing below. One might go so far as to claim that detection is nigh impossible, but that sort of attitude can easily lead to a lack of caution, which is perhaps your worst enemy (other than Alice, the office busybody).

DANGERS TO BE AWARE OF:

- Do not choose a seat that people must pass in order to enter or exit. This is trouble waiting to happen.
- Some managers are on to this trick. Be alert for spies.
- If this meeting will be lengthy, pay enough attention to be prepared for breaks. Anyone paying attention will be eager for breaks, so ignorance of them is a telling sign.
- Look up occasionally, for crying out loud!
- If you are being honored or recognized in any way or must give a presentation, all bets are off. Your distance will actually work against you. Sit close until you are finished and then move to the back if possible. Unfortunately, you may be trapped for the entire meeting.

MEETING ROOMS

These are trickier. Again, the idea is to be as far from the meeting leader as possible. At the far end of the table may be a good place, provided the boss isn't sitting at the other end, which puts you directly in the line of sight. A far corner is best, if it can be arranged. Sitting near like-minded people is a big aid in the deception you need for this to be successful.

Avoid sitting in the boss's line of sight.

DANGERS TO BE AWARE OF:

- Side conversations are a dead giveaway. Each person must be responsible for their own distractions. There are exceptions, which will be covered later.
- You are far more likely to be noticed in these situations. The appearance of attention is of utmost importance.
- Keep your eye on the agenda. Knowing what is going on, even vaguely, will help prevent you from being too lost to fake it if needed.

Side conversations may draw unwanted attention to you.

If you yawn loudly, you are suspect.

ATTITUDE

It is a well-known principle that people who look as though they are supposed to be doing what they are doing are far more likely to get away with what they're doing. For example, a thief who looks around nervously brings attention to him or herself, whereas someone who walks off with their quarry as though they were expected to be carrying it away fits in with peoples' perceptions and is therefore invisible after a fashion. If you look like you want to avoid the meeting, if you yawn loudly or sigh frequently, you are automatically suspect. It's hard to be critical of the motives of someone who seems interested and involved. You must cultivate just the right amount of enthusiasm without looking like a lunatic. This takes some practice, and may at first lead people to believe you a bit off.

To begin with, you need a sense of priority. Maybe there are portions of the meeting that really are important to you. Use these to your benefit by displaying your involvement. Ask pertinent questions, make insightful comments, offer some alternative takes – since you are invested, you may as well make the most of it. It's difficult for people to accuse you of inattention when you have been so actively at the forefront. In fact, some hint of over-enthusiasm might actually result in requests for you to tone it down a little. Now things are right where you want them.

Eye contact is critical. If all anyone sees of you is the top of your head, you have given yourself away. Don't make maniacal, stalker eye contact. A few seconds here and there are sufficient. The most beneficial eye contact will be with the meeting organizer, and whoever is currently speaking. An occasional glance around the table from time to time is excellent for looking engaged.

Make eye contact but don't look maniacal.

The occasional nod plays into the ego of the speaker. Watch longtime sycophants and suck-ups utilize this technique; most have mastered it some time ago. You can learn a great deal from them, but remember that your intentions are markedly different. They are seeking approval, while you are attempting to maintain your sanity. Once you head down their road, you are no longer fit for polite society. "Meeting survivor" is quite a different breed from "person everyone wants to punch repeatedly in the face".

Intermittent participation is vital. You may comment on a particular statement, agree with a proposal, ask seemingly innocent yet subversive questions, or perhaps even praise a specific idea from a coworker. If it is your regular practice to disagree with Bob, go ahead and do so. Conversely, agreeing with him on rare occasions may cause people to remember your participation because of the rarity of the occurrence. Don't overdo it; few people respect gushers, and a sudden and wildly divergent change of behavior will surely raise eyebrows. Remember, you want to be as discrete as you can be and still seem involved. Some useful phrases, to be used with economy, are:

- What are the downsides?
- Do you see any problems with implementation?
- I was thinking the same thing.
- That's an original approach. (Don't sound sarcastic!)
- We did that at the last place I worked.
- That has its advantages.
- I can see where that might work.
- What does everyone else think?
- How will that affect quality?

Again, some level of attention is necessary for these to function properly. Saying "I was thinking the same thing" right after the boss says "Maybe I'm wrong…" may not go well for you.

Make statements that give the appearance that you are interested.

DISTRACTIONS

Now that we've discussed the importance of location and attitude, we will move on to what you can actually do once these considerations have been made. We live in a wonderful technological age where electronics can provide an almost infinite variety of ways to take your mind off the soul-killing activities occurring in meetings. Tablets, smartphones and laptops offer connections to a range of outside diversions for anyone with the intelligence to use them properly. If you are in a responsible position, especially blessed with an organization-supplied device, you are even better off; it is almost expected that you look down from time to time in order to keep on top of whatever task you are in the middle of, or to monitor fires that need to be put out. A clever person will prepare in advance with comments about waiting for an email, expecting a call, or anticipating the figures that will be needed for the meeting. Setting the stage for interruptions is a valuable tool, but it must be cultivated ahead of time for full effect.

In this same vein, email and texts among co-conspirators or people not present at the meeting may also be utilized. Again, technology has opened vast arenas for sweet, sweet distraction. Passing electronic notes and comments between like-minded individuals is often helpful in preserving your endurance, particularly in marathon sessions. Once more, you must be judicious in the usage of such ploys, as looking down constantly may raise the suspicions of those best left ignorant. Sudden bursts of ill-timed laughter may also lead to discovery, embarrassment or possibly even disciplinary action, particularly if the message in question contains what some may deem to be "inappropriate" or "non-pc" elements. Additionally, it is vital that you have the proper notification set. A re-occurring ping or buzz gives away the farm and you will henceforth be under guard for the rest of your tenure; you might as well start looking for a new job now. The vibrate setting may seem like a good idea, but if your device is on a table or some similar surface, it will rattle and migrate across said surface, thereby negating any subtlety you may have exercised to this point.

Questions regarding facts are your friends; they give you the opportunity to volunteer to access the information needed (another reason to pay at least nominal attention in any circumstance). As long as no one is looking at your screen, who knows what you are actually looking at/for? For fullest effectiveness, go into the meeting already aware of any information that may need to be located. If you go in with the information already on screen, a simple minimization means that you can easily look at other sites, pages or documents while the boss believes you are diligently providing a valuable service to the meeting. A few "almost loaded!" declarations allow for precious extra seconds to check your stocks or fantasy sports statistics. The godsend of technology cannot be understated, but it must also be respected. Failure to provide the promised data will invariably result in unwanted scrutiny.

Technology can offer beneficial distraction opportunities.

Another diversion is puzzles: crossword, Jumble, Sudoku, Cryptoquip, etc. There is a serious danger with these distractions, however. Any puzzle worth its salt takes a certain degree of nominal concentration, which may interfere with the all-important task of paying limited attention. It is all too easy to become caught up in the intricacies of a game, and being called three times before responding is a sure way to ruin the venture for yourself, and possibly those around you as well. Please see the previous remarks regarding being a spoiler and being punched repeatedly in the face.

Finally, doodling or sketching is a method frequently employed by many to help stave off boredom. With the rise of tests such as Myers-Briggs, it has become fashionable to accept that different personality types have different styles of working, learning, paying attention, etc. This is an excellent situation for meeting survival, and one is forced to suspect that Ms. Briggs and Ms. Myers were not in fact setting out to categorize personality traits, but rather ensuring that humanity was provided a defense against the onslaught of the modern work environment. Hats off to you, ladies. No doubt you perfected it during a meeting.

As in other circumstances some attention must be paid to the proceedings in order for this to be credible. Additionally, your doodles may be seen by others and so must remain appropriate for a work setting. Drawing your boss or Alice the busybody as a frog, demon or jackass will most certainly backfire on you. If you have rivals, nemeses or spiteful workplace enemies, avoid giving them visible, documented ammunition to use against you. Although temporarily amusing to you, it could become permanent amusement for someone else. Still, some use of discretion and intelligence will allow you to salvage at least a few moments of sanity in an otherwise insane environment.

Your doodles may backfire on you so be careful.

CAMOUFLAGE

This is a corollary to distraction theory. Hiding the true nature of your activities is extremely important. If you are using puzzles or games, for instance, a clipboard angled slightly upward and away from attendees can be seen by others as diligent note-taking. Hiding such things beneath actual meeting-related paperwork can also serve as simple deception, since scrambling around as though searching for relevant information could make you appear to be furiously interested. Keep in mind, however, that puzzles are easily recognized as such, so shuffling requires skill and practice in order to prevent others from seeing even a portion of what you are "working" on.

Puzzles can be covered by paper but also easily recognized

Has the situation become so tedious that you simply must step away to keep from screaming? This can be done, and done with some frequency, but it requires preparation. A large container of the liquid of your choice brought into the meeting is perfect cover for occasional trips out of the room. Everyone can see your healthy efforts to remain hydrated, and what cold-hearted monster would deny a fellow human being the right to relieve themselves as obviously needed?

Frequent hydration can provide opportunities to step out occasionally.

Don't fake it; fill that puppy to the rim and throw that fluid back the entire time you are trapped. This has the additional healthy benefit of actually keeping you hydrated. When you leave the room (and you WILL leave the room!), remember to refill your cup/glass/canteen/thermos/stein before returning so as to perpetuate your natural and excusable periodic departures. Opaque containers as opposed to clear ones work best to camouflage the actual level of liquid contained at any one time. DON'T use alcohol; the problems involved should be readily apparent. Although we all know how much more enjoyable the meeting would be, this short-term pleasure will have long-term consequences which, admittedly, may get you out of all future meetings. And benefits. And paychecks. And subsequent employment. If you just want to be stupid there is no help for you in these pages. Remember, this is about *survival*.

BEST OF LUCK TO YOU!

You, and you alone, will be the judge of how and when to employ these survival techniques. Although the vast majority of meetings are appallingly similar, each will nevertheless have its own unique challenges, logistics, characteristics, demographics, environment and pitfalls. The author cannot be responsible for wildly inappropriate usage of the suggestions outlined above. You know your situation; make the most of that knowledge.

Now you are ready. Good luck!

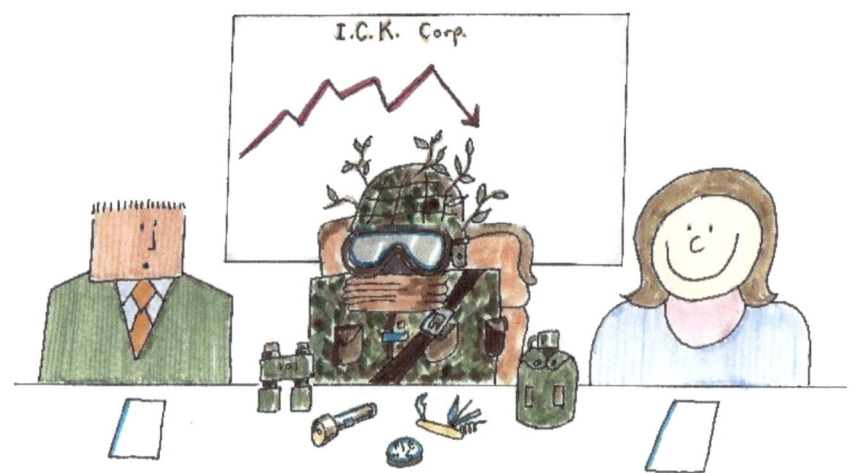

OTHER BOOKS BY
VIC PARRISH & STEPHEN JACKSON

If Dogs Had Pockets

Harry Goatee Is Hungry

The Bear in My Bedroom

I Had Such A Wonderful Day

The Stairwell That Nobody Knows

The Great Cupcake War

www.ingramcontent.com/pod-product-compliance
Lightning Source LLC
Chambersburg PA
CBHW040254220526
45473CB00001B/480